Oodles of Writing Activities

Written by Linda Milliken
Typography and Design by Lorraine Stegman
Edited by Kathy Rogers
Cover Design by Wendy Loreen
Cover Art by Patty McCloskey

Using the Book:

Integrate writing into your curriculum by selecting from a wide variety of topics and suggestions.

OR introduce the sections in order to expose students to the progression of writing.

Contents:

Oodles of Writing Activities • © 1998 Edupress • PO Box 883 • Dana Point, CA 92629
ISBN 1-56472-002-0

Writing Environments

A classroom environment that encourages writing will help students become more comfortable, enthusiastic writers.

Here are some suggestions to help create a good writing environment.

Provide lots of experiences:

Go on observation walks and field trips. Talk about what you saw and did.

Do lots of "hands-on" projects. Ask students to talk about what they're doing and how they're doing it.

Ask speakers, parents and guests to visit the classroom and talk to the children. Encourage children to ask questions.

Feature writing prominently on bulletin boards. Some all-purpose headings are:

"We all have something to say."   "Writing Wizards"

"Your thoughts count in here."   "Authors' Alley"

"Glorious Stories"   "Writing Roundup"

Encourage the verbal exchange of thoughts and ideas. Be sure to let students know there are no right or wrong answers—only possibilities.

Develop a listening area complete with individual headsets and a variety of tapes—music, stories, sounds and so on. Ask them to share their reactions with friends in the center.

Turn an area into a "Description Center." Stock it with items such as seashells, decals, buttons, miniatures, pictures and so on. Children can bring items from home to add. Visit the center in pairs and take turns choosing an item and describing it to the other child.

Provide opportunity for simple, ungraded free-time writing:

Put a "Suggestion Box" on your desk. Make sure you read and act upon the suggestions. Let students know their ideas count!

Create a writing center that changes with the seasons, holiday or curriculum. Fill the center with ideas from our "Story Starter" section. Make the presentation creative. A bow-adorned basket can be filled with Easter story starters; a pumpkin can be hollowed and stuffed with Halloween or Thanksgiving ideas.

Tack a large piece of butcher paper to the wall, write a headline on it and set a can of pencils nearby for "on the spot" jotting of thoughts and ideas. Here are some headline ideas:

So you're not feeling well…a spot for get-well messages for an ailing classmate.

Just a note to…could be the principal, someone who visited the class or anyone else who comes to mind.

Birthday Board…a super large greeting card for that special birthday person.

Complainer's Corner…have a complaint about something? Share it!

Advice Column…children write anonymous letters asking for advice on a problem or question. Others answer at the bottom.

News Notes…post pictures and current events. Children write their opinions.

Give students an opportunity to write just for themselves:

Make personalized journals where they can privately record thoughts about the day, an event, or feelings.

Provide tape recorders. Let children tape their thoughts and play the tape back for themselves. After they listen to their thoughts played back they can erase the tape.

Oodles of Writing Activities © *Edupress*

Experience First

Provide classroom experiences that foster imaginative thinking, stimulate conversation and serve as springboards to writing.

Field trips:
Plan together . . . evaluate afterwards.

Films:
Discuss reactions, summarize contents, share questions.

Guests:
Interview, talk about occupations and interests.

Travel brochures and maps:
Locate places, take imaginary trips, research interesting facts.

Music:
Close your eyes and visualize the music. What do you see?

Observation walks:
Notice changes, be alert to sounds and sights. Talk about what you saw.

Art projects:
Describe your creation. Talk about the process involved.

Art:
Discuss the work of great artists. Describe what you see.

Sense adventures:
Get kids in touch with their senses. Look through colored cellophane. Take blindfold walks. Close your eyes and describe only what you hear. Sample foods and describe textures.

Current events:
Discuss the contents. Compare reactions.

Stories and books:
Talk about the characters. Make up some of your own.

Photographs:
Describe the background. Note the settings. Are there people in it? How do they look–tired, happy?

Talk-about Topics

Before you put pencil to paper, get rid of writing fears by "writing" orally. When kids learn that writing is simply putting on paper what you want to say they will feel more comfortable.

Here are some topics to talk about:

Early memories:

What do you think you were good at the first
  day you were born?
What's the first memory you have?
Share a funny story your parents have told
  you about you.

More about you:

Brag about something you can do well.
Where would you like to go on vacation?
What are your hobbies and interests?
Tell about a special event in your life.
What kinds of things do you worry about?

School things:

If you were a teacher what would you do?
Make up some playground rules.
Describe the perfect playground.

In the news:

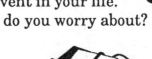

Who is your favorite actress? singer? athlete?
What can you tell about the news stories of the day?
If you were President, what would you do first?
What kind of weather do you prefer?

All year long:

Discuss your best memory about an upcoming
  holiday.
What is your favorite season?
Do you like your birthday? Why or why not?
At what age should we stop celebrating
  birthdays?
What's the best way to celebrate a birthday?

Free time things:

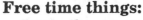

Do you have a special stuffed animal or toy?
What sport do you like best?
What should people do for relaxation?
What's a good way to make friends?
Which is better . . . movies, television or radio?
What are your favorite movies? songs? television
  shows?

5

Solution Resolutions

Problem solving lays the groundwork for plot development. Students learn that there may be several viewpoints and solutions to every situation and problem.

Pose these problems to the group then open up discussion. Encourage creativity, logic and freedom of expression.

The subject is . . .

Safety

- Your friends are doing something you think is dangerous.

- Someone you don't know tries to strike up a conversation with you on the street.

Friendship

- You want to give your friend a gift but you have no money.

- Someone is picking on you at school.

- Your best friend won't talk to you.

Personal Stuff

- You've forgotten your homework.

- You need a special new outfit for a one-night school performance.

- You have a problem at home you're afraid to share.

- Your messy brother won't keep his half of the room clean.

Conservation

- The amount of litter after school lunches is growing.

- You're at someone's house for dinner and you don't like what they're serving.

- You need to cut down on the use of electricity at home.

Lost and Found

- You see someone with something you know is yours.

- You found $10 on the playground.

- You're lost in a shopping center.

Pets and Things

- You're too embarrassed to take your favorite stuffed animal to a friend's to spend the night.

- Your pet followed you to school.

- Your pet dug up the neighbor's flower garden looking for a bone.

- Your special pet died.

THINKER THINGS

Put your thoughts into words.

What do you think . . .

about eating cake for breakfast

about homework

is the scariest animal

about the tooth fairy

of the rain

about baseball

about spiders

causes goosepimples

is the yukkiest vegetable

is the best holiday

about being an adult

we should do today

Rather bes . .

Which would you rather be? Tell why.

a snowflake or a raindrop

a king or a subject

a movie star or a fan

a hunter or prey

a pirate or a cowboy

a dog or a cat

a mouse or a chicken

a lion or a snake

a boy or a girl

a vegetable or a candy bar

a train or a plane

a star or a cloud

thunder or lightning

appetizer or dessert

What's the difference between . . .

a shoe box and a box of shoes

a hot dog and a hamburger

a desert and a dessert

a bath and a shower

morning and night

soup and jello

sunrise and sunset

laughing and crying

a shout and a whisper

friends and enemies

breakfast and dinner

work and play

television and radio

water and ice

outdoors and indoors

sailing and rowing

Oodles of Writing Activities © *Edupress*

IN YOUR OWN WORDS

Find pictures of different animals and mount them on cardboard. Place several on the chalk rail.

Choose one student to describe one of the pictures without telling which one it is. Note size, color, and body parts such as eyes, tail, ears. Ask another child to point to the one being described.

This activity can also be done with pictures of food, cars, people and scenes, all cut from magazines.

Write a noun on a 3x5 index card. Put all cards in a container. Pass the container. A student pulls a card and describes the word on the card. How long does it take the class to guess the noun?

Some suggested words: horse, car, butterfly, boat, turkey, socks, stove, king, globe, bee, cactus, seed, saw, hammer. As students improve in ability the difficulty of the words can increase.

Hold up an article of clothing. Ask students to describe it. Note color, print, buttons, snaps, size, shape, holes, patches, and so on.

Let me tell you all about . . .

Learn To List

Listing is a form of categorizing. Start with just a word and you can wind up with many that mean the same or express another way of saying the word. To give you an idea of how to list follow these instructions.

Write the headings on the chalkboard. Read the words. Ask students under which heading the word should be placed. Older students can do this as a written assignment.

WORDS:

error	gang	troop	knock	scrub
mob	launder	rap	goof	confuse
throng	immaculate	boo-boo	pop	crunch
band	spotless	mix-up	mop	crash
herd	wash	bumble	throng	bathe

HEADINGS:

clean	crowd	mistake	sound

Oodles of Writing Activities © *Edupress*

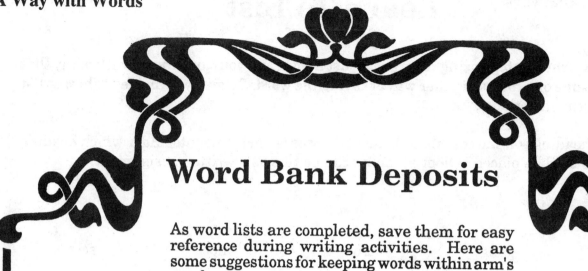

Word Bank Deposits

As word lists are completed, save them for easy reference during writing activities. Here are some suggestions for keeping words within arm's reach.

Individual student lists:

Copy words on index cards by category, subject and word types. Store in index box files to keep on each desk.

Copy words on index cards. Clearly mark the category at the top. Laminate, punch a hole in the corner and slide onto shower curtain rings. Hang the rings from each chair.

Fill photo albums with index card word lists instead of pictures.

Classroom lists:

Create a "wall of words." Hang butcher paper strips ceiling to floor. Start at the top and keep the lists going throughout the school year. Kids can decorate with appropriate pictures or stickers.

Word Centers: Develop a "word center" filled with rhyming dictionaries, books about word origins and meanings, dictionaries, maps and thesauruses.

Attach a class-created word list to hangers and hang from a rack built from dowels. Label each list clearly. As students need a word they can take a list off the rack.

List Assists

Change the format of listing lessons to keep interest high.
Here are some ways to do just that!

List Hook-ups

Each new entry repeats or utilizes some part of the idea given last:

- The new word begins with the last letter of the previous word.

- The new word begins with the next letter of the alphabet.

- The words follow a spelling pattern: for example, 3-letter, 4-letter, 5-letter words, then back to 3 letters.

- The words follow a category pattern: for example, if the list subject is transportation the words are added in this order—land, sea, air transportation.

Round-about Lists

Sit in a circle. Pick a topic. Travel round the circle, each student offering a word to add to the list. When someone gets stuck, go on to the next. Maybe they'll be ready when their turn comes round again.

This could be made competitive by eliminating students who are unable to add to the list.

Word Scavengers

Choose a list topic. Set out in pairs with notebook and pencil. Ask all you meet to add to the list. Regroup with classmates and compile a master list. Keep a tally. Which word was offered most often? Least often? Which is the most unusual?

Lists On the Horizon

Choose the list topic. Write the words horizontally on a roll of calculator tape. Continue to unroll the tape and secure it to the wall around the classroom as words are added. How many days does it take to complete the tape?

A Way with Words

Here are some ideas for word lists. And this is just the beginning . . .

LOCATIONS:
types of buildings/dwellings
vacation destinations
countries
geographic features
cities
states
continents
provinces

RECREATION:
toys
sports
games
hobbies
activities

PEOPLE:
nationalities
occupations
handicaps
famous
physical characteristics
temperament
kinds (giant,etc.)

DESCRIPTIONS:
Other ways to say . . .

wet	pretty	happy
sticky	smart	tired
creepy	ugly	sad
mean	dirty	scared
funny	sharp	mad
fast	crazy	quiet
dangerous	grouchy	many
big	exciting	fun

Loads of Lists

ACTION:
Other words to describe . . .

walk	like
run	dislike
fix	love
break	clean
laugh	argue
speak	cry
look	play

SUBJECT:
colors
animals
    wild, pets, animal houses
inventions
inventors
weapons
measurement
holidays
transportation
shapes
creatures, monsters
space
medicine
music
time
trees
plants
flowers
insects
weather
school
cooking
eras in history
clothing
costumes
art
birds
types of adventures
tools
food
    desserts
    fruits, vegetables, etc.
    textures
birds

"Me" Lists

Think about the things you do and the different ways you feel. Personal experience
is helpful information for story writing.

List...

YOU

Things you
think are...

silly
icky
wonderful
exciting
disappointing
weird
shabby
important
clever
cozy
mysterious
challenging

FAVORITE THINGS

Colors you like
Colors you dislike

Things that
make you...

laugh
cry
proud
sorry
jump
nervous
argue
tremble
frustrated
smile
grumpy

MOMENTS

an embarrassing
moment
a distressing moment
a lonely moment
a dynamic moment

Things that make
you say...

"Yes!"
"No!"
"Maybe."

Things you...

hate to do   hate to see
love to do   love to see

hate to eat   hate to wear
love to eat   love to wear

MEMORIES
a super memory
an awful memory
an exciting memory

NAMES YOU WISH
WERE YOURS

What Does That Mean?

Silly or made-up words can be used to spice up a story. Imagine if someone found a thingamajig! What could it be? It's up to your imagination.

Here are some silly words. Some do exist and some are made-up. Write your own definition or description for each word.

1. bamboozle _____

2. humdrum _____

3. doohickey _____

4. thingamajig _____

5. gizmo _____

6. cascarilla _____

7. cattywampus _____

8. jabberwocky _____

9. tintinnabulation _____

10. tinkerminny _____

11. wahooly _____

12. raffinose _____

13. sweetitis _____

14. knackerwood _____

Which ones do you think are really words? Look in your dictionary.

Now add two of your own. Find one silly word in the dictionary and make one up.

1. _____

2. _____

Words That Make Sense

Your senses provide many words to add to your growing vocabulary!

EXTERNAL SENSES

Hearing
List words to describe the sound of . . .
- a bell
- wind
- thunder
- rain
- the ocean
- birdcalls
- a footstep
- fire
- a horn
- noises

List things that relate to your ears
List things that cover your ears

Sight
List words that describe . . .
- types of vision
- eye coverings
- parts of the eye
- a sunset
- a sunrise
- a diamond

List ways the eye feels
List things that get in your eyes

Smell
List pleasant smells
List unpleasant smells
List things your nose can do
List ways to smell and breathe
List words that describe smells

Taste
List words that describe . . .
- the way things taste
- ways to taste (drink, sip, etc.)

List things that are . . .
- chewy
- tough
- bitter
- sweet

Touch
List words that describe . . .
- textures
- temperatures
- physical gestures

INTERNAL SENSES

List words to describe . . .
- hunger
- pain
- thirst
- fatigue

List words related to . . .
- muscles
- the brain
- changes in the body

Everything's Relative

Write at least three words you can think of that relate to (have something to do with) the words below. The first is done for you.

pencil: _lead, write, eraser, wood, sharpen, point_____

dentist: _____

birthday: _____

breakfast: _____

zoo: _____

baseball: _____

rain: _____

bedtime: _____

hamburger: _____

school: _____

ocean: _____

baby: _____

sun: _____

mountain: _____

city: _____

Rewrite It

Rewrite the phrase and use another word that means the same or close to the same thing in place of the **BOLD** word.

Here's an example:

an **amazing** invention ___a startling invention_____

---

a **pretty** young lady _____

a **daring** pirate _____

a **cute** puppy _____

a **creepy** noise _____

a **strong** wind _____

a noisy **crowd** _____

a bumpy **road** _____

a cool **creek** _____

a **big** house _____

a **dark** cave _____

a **hurt** knee _____

a **super** idea _____

a scary **monster** _____

a **grumbling** brother _____

a **strong** man _____

                    Oodles of Writing Activities © *Edupress*

Start With a Sentence

Finish these thoughts.

1. I hate it when _____.

2. I love it when _____.

3. I get mad when _____.

4. It isn't fair that _____.

5. I laughed when _____.

6. I cried when _____.

7. I felt scared when _____.

8. I don't believe that _____.

9. I wish I could _____.

10. If I could go anywhere _____.

11. If I could change my name _____.

12. I really enjoy _____.

13. I like to think about _____.

14. If I could be an animal _____.

Choose one of the sentences. Write three more to go with it.
You have a paragraph!

I'd Like to Know . . .

Write 3 questions you would ask if you were going to interview . . .

the first man to walk on the moon

1. _____

2. _____

3. _____

King Kong

1. _____

2. _____

3. _____

the President or Prime Minister of your country

1. _____

2. _____

3. _____

the heavyweight boxing champion of the world

1. _____

2. _____

3. _____

your great-great grandmother

1. _____

2. _____

3. _____

an invisible man

1. _____

2. _____

3. _____

Oodles of Writing Activities © *Edupress*

Two Minutes of Your Time

Pick a topic each day—the writing time limit is two minutes. This activity encourages spontaneous thinking and writing that doesn't need editing.

Which would you rather be and why?
- magician, pirate or king
- adult, child, grandparent
- tall or short
- fireman or policeman
- 10 feet tall or 2 feet tall
- by yourself or with a group
- awake or asleep
- famous or unknown
- bath or shower

How would you cure ...
- a giraffe with the hiccups
- the common cold
- sore muscles
- an elephant with a toothache
- an ape with a headache
- chattering teeth
- goose bumps
- laryngitis

Write about ways you can ...
- be helpful
- be a good friend
- be organized
- have fun
- relax
- cook eggs
- eat ice cream

What would you do with ...
- a dragon in your bathtub
- one million dollars
- a 300 pound pickle
- a two-foot long hotdog
- a plane ticket to anywhere
- a ton of bubblegum
- 30 gallons of hot fudge
- a cloud of soapsuds

Create different uses for ...
- paper clip
- button
- sponge
- towel
- soap
- scotch tape
- toothbrush
- hair gel
- egg yolks
- spatula

Imaginings

How would it feel to be a cloud?
You're a camera—what do you like to take pictures of the most?
You live in a palace. What's it like?

Photo Presentations

Put a different photo or magazine picture in a picture frame each day. Pick one of these 2-minute writing exercises:

write silly captions   describe everything you see
make up a story plot   describe the setting

You're not yourself today...

Imagine you're an object, animal or insect. What can you do? How do you feel? What experiences might be fun and interesting for you? How would other animals and people treat you? Where could you be found?

You're not yourself you're a...

raindrop	football	school bus
rubberband	carrot	guitar
shopping cart	telescope	foot
garbage disposal	bandaid	mouth
pencil	tornado	earthquake
onion	banana	diary
birthday cake	snowflake	sailboat
candle	river	tumbleweed
flower	snowman	telephone
microscope	automobile	spaceship
pancake	sunrise	star
tunnel	frying pan	dollar bill
wheel	teddy bear	suitcase

You're not yourself you're a...

giraffe	elephant	seagull
worm	bumblebee	butterfly
mule	woodpecker	bat
cow	anteater	crocodile
lion	snake	camel
frog	whale	jellyfish
alley cat	poodle	gorilla
polar bear	kangaroo	sow bug
turtle	mouse	horse
swan	skunk	octopus
snail	porcupine	parrot
mosquito	firefly	buffalo
rooster	dinosaur	lizard

Oodles of Writing Activities © *Edupress*

EXAGGERATION CONGLOMERATION

Have you ever heard the expression, "It was so hot I could have fried an egg on the sidewalk!" Finish these phrases with an exaggeration:

It was so cold . . .

The raindrops were so big . . .

It was so long . . .

The child was so dirty . . .

It was so windy . . .

The sky was so blue . . .

I was so happy . . .

The night was so dark . . .

He was so strong . . .

The cat was so fat . . .

He was so brave . . .

The house was so big . . .

She was so pretty . . .

The car was so old . . .

The man was so tall . . .

She was so rich . . .

He was so tiny . . .

The dog barked so loud . . .

I was so full . . .

The joke was so funny . . .

The monster was so ugly . . .

My teacher was so mad . . .

Sometimes we exaggerate about what we can do. For example, "His nose was so big he could smell a cake baking on the other side of town!" Finish the phrase with an exaggerated accomplishment.

He was so smart he could . . .

His mouth was so big . . .

She jumped so high she could . . .

Her voice was so loud . . .

She ran so fast she could . . .

Use your imagination to conjure up some wild exaggerations. Write a paragraph that describes . . .

The biggest sandwich you ever ate.

The scariest thing you've ever seen.

The loudest noise you've ever heard.

The bumpiest thing you've ever touched.

The smelliest thing you've ever smelled.

A **TALL** Tale is a story that stretches the truth about the abilities of the main character. Read about Paul Bunyan and Pecos Bill to find out more about legendary heroes and tall tales.

Write a paragraph that exaggerates an accomplishment of one of the characters created below. Remember, you need to decide what the character could do well. Then make up an amazing feat accomplished as a result of the character's skill. For example:

> Cowboy Bob was the best roper on the range. One day he was rounding up a herd of buffalo when there was a great stampede. So Cowboy Bob swung his great rope, let it fly and lassoed the entire herd all at once. Ever since that day the other cowboys saluted when Bob rode by!

Now let's hear all about . . .

Pistol Pete	Bullfighter Bill
Cowgirl Kate	Len the Lumberjack
Safari Sue	Sam the Sea Captain
Policeman Pat	Chief Sitting Tall
Explorer Ed	Big Game Hunter Hal
Detective Dan	Knowlin the Knight
Stagecoach Seth	Fast-foot Freddy
Bronco Bob	Mountain Man Mack
Rough Ridin' Ralph	Desert Don
Truck Drivin' Tess	Firefighter Frank

CONQUERING CONVERSATION

It's not easy to write dialogue! Try some of these conversational activities. Start simply but be sure quotation marks and punctuation marks are placed correctly.

Silly Statements

Try your hand at these one-line conversations. Here's an example: What did the hot fudge say to the ice cream? "I'm so hot you'll melt when you see me!"

What did the . . .

ball say to the bat?

shoe say to the foot?

elephant say to the ant?

pencil say to the paper?

dog say to the cat?

sun say to the moon?

bird say to the tree?

mouth say to the ear?

bee say to the flower?

cracker say to the cheese?

hammer say to the nail?

fish say to the bait?

cookie say to the milk?

mountain say to the bulldozer?

hat say to the head?

Situation Say-so

What would you say in a situation and how would you say it? Use your expression "word bank" to help you. Follow the example:

Situation
      a dark, quiet theater
"I can't find a seat," I whispered.

a noisy football game

being chased by a large dog

being picked on by a bully

want to spend the night at a friend's

just saw a ghost

got off at the wrong bus stop

just won a race

stepped on a bee

heard a funny joke

didn't finish your homework

Open and Closed Case

Write short endings for each of these mini-stories.

At first the noise seemed far away. It was an odd noise, one that the boys didn't recognize. As the sound moved closer they went out to see what it might be.

_____

_____

_____

Today was a sunny day, just the sort of day I like. I packed a lunch and telephoned my best friend. "Let's go on an adventure bike ride," I said. He agreed. So we got on our bikes and headed

_____

_____

_____

One evening, when the sun had set and the sky was already dark, I was standing just listening to the night sounds. Suddenly, as I looked in amazement, something brilliant flashed through the sky and landed in the field not far from my house. I ran to see what it was.

_____

_____

_____

Snowball was a fluffy white kitten. She was always doing silly things and getting into trouble. One day we had to go out of town. Snowball was left alone all day, by herself, in the house. When we got back we were anxious to see how Snowball had done while we were away. We opened the front door carefully and went in the house.

_____

_____

_____

Oodles of Writing Activities © *Edupress*

Paragraph Patter

Here are some ideas for writing "just a paragraph"

Superlatives

The loudest noise I ever heard
The biggest problem I have
The best television show
The most important thing in my lfe
The prettiest sight I've seen
The most delicious dessert

The perfect…

meal	day	birthday cake
friend	school	pet
bedroom	mother	toy
teacher	father	vacation
pizza		

Good Idea or Bad Idea? Why?

Walking in the rain   Belonging to a club
Watching television   Having just one friend
Eating candy   Breaking a promise
Keeping a secret   Going to school when you're sick
Eating pizza for breakfast   Eating pancakes for dinner
Sharing a favorite game or toy   Tattling on someone

"I" Stuff

I worry about…   I don't like to…
I hope I'll never…   I like to play…
I wish people wouldn't…   I wonder why…
I feel bad when…   I would like to go to…
I am bothered by…   I would like to learn how…
I get grouchy when…   I always remember…

"Friend" Stuff

The best quality in a friend
The worst quality in a friend
A good way to make a new friend
If a friend hurt my feelings…
A good gift from a friend

Complainer's Corner

The most irritating job I have to do
The sound that bugs me the most
I think it's ridiculous that…
If I could complain about just one thing…
I don't understand why…
My parents are wrong when…

Paragraph Patter

Just "Stuff"

My favorite stuffed animal
The night I slept over at my friend's house
If I could meet anyone in the world…
Happiness is…
The best ride at an amusement park is…
My favorite cartoon character
The oldest person I know
It's a mistake to…
A baby needs…
My favorite kind of cookie
The musical instrument I would like to play
If I could have a dozen of something it would be…
If I could have any gift in the world I would want…

"Silly Stuff"

The silliest-looking vegetable
A silly idea
A silly experience
A silly dream

Of Interest

An interesting place to visit
An interesting person I know
An interesting book

Double Explanations
Pick two to describe:

Double trouble
Double header
Double-cross
Double-time
Double-jointed
Double-decker

Everything I know about…

baking a cake
a hippopotamus
being a good friend
pitching a tent
driving an automobile
an airplane
building a house
planting a garden
taking care of a dog
the desert

Just For Openers

The first sentence of a story should make the reader curious and want to read more!

For example:
As he stepped up to the starting line and looked at the crowd he saw something that made him tingle with fear!

Do you want to know more? What did he see? The possibilities are endless and you will find out only by reading on.

Finish these opening sentences. Ask yourself, "If I were the reader would I want to read more?"

1. When I looked under my pillow to see what the tooth fairy left _____

_____

2. One moment after the spaceship was launched we _____

_____

3. As the scientist looked through his microscope _____

_____

4. The boys carefully went into the opening of the _____

_____

5. She opened the box _____

_____

6. They were sleeping snugly inside the tent when _____

_____

7. The day started just like any other day until _____

_____

Tell two things that could happen in a story about:

1. two boys on a sailboat

_____

_____

2. running a marathon

_____

_____

3. a camping trip

_____

_____

4. a day at the beach

_____

_____

5. a train trip across the Rocky Mountains

_____

_____

6. diving for a ship that sank

_____

_____

7. life on a farm

_____

_____

8. a terrible blizzard

_____

_____

9. a safari through Africa

_____

_____

10. your first day in a new school

_____

Create a Character

Use the worksheet on the following page to create a character for one or more of these suggested story settings.

... a wagon train on a journey through Indian country. (helpful hints: a scout, an Indian chief)

... a police station.

... a secluded cabin high in the mountains.

... a tropical island in the Pacific Ocean.

... an expedition to the Antarctic.

... the kitchen of a world-famous restaurant.

... a second-grade classroom.

... a castle in the time of knights and dragons.

... the control tower of a busy airport.

... a 3-ring, traveling circus.

... a school for handicapped children.

... a professional baseball camp for rookies.

... the largest cruise ship in the world.

... a newly-discovered planet.

... a farm.

... a doctor's office.

Create a Character

Character's Name _____

Male _____ Female _____ Animal _____ Other _____

Physical characteristics:

eyes _____   hair _____

height _____   weight _____

Three words that best describe this character <u>physically</u>:
(For example: large, muscular, handsome, etc.)

_____   _____   _____

Other distinctive characteristics: (Limps when he walks, etc.)

_____

_____

Personal qualities:
List at least four. (For example: brave, clever, quiet, shy)

_____   _____

_____   _____

Abilities:
Can this character do anything unusual? Has the character accomplished anything unique? Any interests or hobbies?

_____

_____

_____

Personal information:
Describe family, occupation and any other information that is important to the story.

_____

_____

_____

Detail Development

Be able to picture sentences in your mind—as if you were looking at a photograph. Rewrite the sentences. Add detail to make sentences that "show". You should be able to draw a picture to go with your sentence. For example:

I felt a pain in my stomach.
My stomach ached so much I was doubled over with pain.

Now it's your turn:

1. The dog ran fast.

   _____

2. My grandparents are old.

   _____

3. It was dark outside.

   _____

4. It snowed very hard.

   _____

5. The man wore a tie.

   _____

6. The children dressed for a winter day.

   _____

7. Many clouds were in the sky.

   _____

8. They sat down to eat dinner.

   _____

9. A tiger sprang from the bushes.

   _____

10. She got a package in the mail.

    _____

Sensational Settings

Here's the character. You set the scene. The first one is done for you. Use at least four descriptive words.

EXAMPLE: a pilot . . . in an out-of-control helicopter. _____

a cowboy _____

a sheriff _____

an acrobat _____

a doctor _____

a caterpillar _____

a king _____

an astronaut _____

Frankenstein _____

a magician _____

a musician _____

a caveman _____

a lion _____

a wrestler _____

a pharoah _____

a baseball player _____

Oodles of Writing Activities © *Edupress*

The setting is an important part of a story because it tells us where and when a story takes place. The choices are only as endless as your imagination! And we have the past, present and future in which to place our characters.

Think about the story ideas below. Then create a setting. In the next column tell when the story takes place. If you choose past or future try to be more specific and list a date or historical era.

An example is done for you. Use your wonderful imagination!

A story about ...	SETTING: where	when
1. baseball	Yankee Stadium, New York	the 1920 World Series
2. searching for gold		
3. a robbery		
4. a shipwreck		
5. mountain climbing		
6. an earthquake		
7. sailing		
8. hot-air balloon trip		
9. surfing		
10. hiking		
11. a trip across the desert		
12. a cattle roundup		
13. a special vacation		
14. a tugboat		

Head 'em Up

Headlines and titles play an important part in a story or article. They capture the reader's interest and help tell in a few words what the story or article is about.

Write 5 imaginary headlines you would be likely to see in your newspaper tomorrow.

Look in a newspaper. Read the headlines. Rewrite one.

Rewrite these boring story titles to make new, interesting ones:

The Lost Dog	The Sailboat
A Big Adventure	What I Like About Night
A Trip to the Zoo	The Funny Monkey

Create a title for these story ideas:

- Five boys are stranded in the mountains while on a camping trip. They had only enough food for three days. Their adventure really starts on the fourth. This story is about their survival.

- A town is invaded by a giant tarantula. This story is about how the townspeople got rid of the gigantic spider!

Look through a newspaper. Write down three headlines that caught your interest. Tell why.

Look through the library shelves at school. List three book titles that caught your interest. Tell why.

Create three titles for the same story. Take a poll. Which title is most interesting to your classmates?

Make up a story title for each category:

- a true story
- an adventure story
- a fantasy

WHET YOUR APPETITE

Cook Up a Burger

Cut out hamburger ingredients from construction paper. You'll need:

  2 hamburger buns
  1 hamburger meat patty
  lots of garnish—pickles, onions, tomatoes and cheese for
  starters

Write an opening story sentence on one bun half. Tell about the story plot on the burger patty. Describe the main character on a slice of tomato. List other details— events, settings, support characters—on the remaining garnish. You can add as much garnish as you want. Write a story ending on the other burger bun.

Assemble the burger and glue it to a paper plate or construction paper. Who can build the biggest, juiciest hamburger?

Stuff a Sub

Follow the same concept as for the hamburger but stuff a giant submarine sandwich instead. Different ingredients will represent story parts—try bologna, pastrami, swiss cheese, olives and salami.

Build a Sundae

This story outline unfolds from the scoops, toppings, nuts, whipped cream and cherry. M-m-m good story ideas!

In Disguise

Create costume boxes to use for dress up and role playing or as lead-ins to story writing.

Here are some ideas for the costume bags or boxes:

1
sandals
cape
toy sword

2
goggles
mittens
parka

3
ballet slippers
tutu
whistle

4
coat & tie
briefcase
hat

5
hammer
how-to manual
hard hat

6
nurse's hat
stethoscope
thermometer

7
bedroom slippers
bathrobe
shower cap

8
cowboy hat
vest
boots
rope

9
pajamas
teddy bear

Create entire story plots

Practice writing open sentences
    "He was the wizard of Wall Street."
might be an opener to go with the #4.

Create settings and characters

Make up conversations

10
smock
beret
paint brush

11
sweats
tights

12
apron
menu
chef's hat
order pad

13
skateboard
kneepads
T-shirt
shorts

14
golf shoes
golf ball
trophy

15
gray wig
spectacles
wallet

16
hula skirt
lei
plastic flowers

17
military uniform
world map

18
jogging shorts
tennis shoes
race entry number

Endless Possibilities

WHO

explorer	archaeologist	princess
pilot	eskimo	fisherman
astronaut	3 bears	dinosaur
dragon	skeleton	monster
newborn baby	unicorn	great white whale
detective	cowboy	bullfighter
teeny-tiny witch	pirate	sailor
captain	lion tamer	teacher
penguin	fireman	fearless hunter
chef	artist	carpenter
clown	race car driver	athlete
knight	engineer	giant
ballet dancer	pioneer	doctor
sheriff	bandit	robot
witch doctor	evil emperor	barber
caterpillar	porcupine	flamingo
detective	magician	birdwatcher
neighbors	strangers	teenagers
champion	prisoner	salesman
busybody	butler	bum
dastardly villain	angry mob	cowardly giant
wicked witch	sly wizard	tooth fairy
snoopy neighbor	magical elf	ancient genie
ruthless ruler	brave warrier	kindhearted hippo
bumbling professor	big bully	nurse

Endless Possibilities

WHAT

searching for gold
visiting an old friend
hauling dangerous cargo
solving an ancient riddle
lost at sea
hiding from something
solving a mystery
meeting a stranger
travelling in a strange land
making a brave rescue
solving a problem
on a daring mission
hunting for an unusual animal
making a homer
crossing a raging river
clutching a magic wand
discovering an ancient pyramid
stalking a legendary creature
following a rainbow
causing trouble
nabbing a criminal
risking his/her life
in a tough predicament
waiting
getting bad news
getting good news
making an important announcement

wearing a disguise
learning a secret
facing a great challenge
chasing a runaway train
falling in love
helping a friend
fighting a battle
caught in a tornado
investigating strange noises
beating the odds
exploring a secret passage
casting a spell
winning a contest
attacking the enemy
going to college
making a new friend
battling Mother Nature
visiting the future
visiting the past
stuck in a cave
defending his or her honor
leading an army
delivering an important message
doing his/her favorite thing
fixing something broken
meeting a phantom

Oodles of Writing Activities © *Edupress*

Prop Up a Story

Props make a story come to life as well as serving as imagination motivators.

Add to the fun of these two projects by doing them in small groups of three or four students.

Collect objects such as stuffed animals, toys, dolls and miniature trees, people and buildings.

Each group selects an assortment of objects from the display. These objects are then incorporated into a story.

Remind students they will need a main character, a setting and a plot or problem to be resolved. For example, the story could be about a little girl who has lost her favorite stuffed bear. Where will she look? Perhaps in the woods behind a tall tree. What happens on her search for the bear?

Encourage the story and manipulating the props.

Use magazine pictures to tell a story.

Each person in the group cuts out a picture and pastes it to a piece of tagboard or construction paper.

Create a story based on the pictures. Each child is responsible for narrating that part of the story that is based on his or her picture.

Sound Alikes

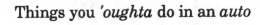

Have some storytelling fun with these ideas from sound-alike words.

Things you *'oughta* do in an *auto*

Adventures of a *bare bear*

Which witch do you know?

Tale of a runaway *tail*

Shopping for *china* in *China*

The best *way* to *weigh* a hippo

The embarrassed *hare* with no *hair*

What *would* you do with 1000 pieces of *wood*?

The *hoarse* talking *horse*

Hey! Look what's in the *hay!*

The day *you* were a *ewe*

What did you do with the *sail* you bought on *sale*?

Whether or not you like changes in the *weather*

How to *heal* a sore *heel*

How you plugged a *leak* with a *leek*

The best way to *haul* bricks down a long *hall*

Why you *bawled* when you lost the *ball*

Why you turned *pale* when you saw what was in the *pail*

The *fourth* time you went *forth* into the mountains

The *fouled*-up *fowl*

Four wishes *for* you

The un*fair fare*

I was a private *eye*

A silly way you *rode* down a *road*

The *two* ballerinas in the fancy *tutus*

What your friend did when you touched his/her *two lips* with a *tulip*

The mysterious *red* diary you *read*

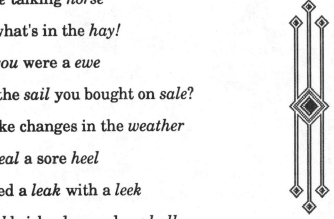

Oodles of Writing Activities © Edupress

TITLE GRABBAG

Fantasy

My Magic Carpet Ride

The Saddest Dragon

Life on a Cloud

The Doll that Came to Life

The Wishing Well

The Talking Stone

The Two-headed Dragon

What the Tooth Fairy Does with the Teeth

Science Fiction

Runaway Robots

Escape to Blue Planet

The UFO

Close Encounter at Sea

Time Machine Trip

Invasion of the Giant Grasshoppers

2000 Years from Today

A Journey Through Space

Historical

Kite Flying with Ben Franklin

The Knight's Best Memory

Wagon Train Adventure

The First Airplane Flight

A Scary Stagecoach Ride

My Log Cabin Home

The Treasure in the Pyramid

Animals

The Angry Alligator

The Gourmet Gorilla

My Pocket Pet

Mr. Penguin for President

The Cow and the Cookie

The Surprise in the Kangaroo's Pouch

The Polka-dot Zebra

Monkey Shenanigans

TITLE GRABBAG

Adventure

The Runaway Train

A Dangerous Mission

Rescue at Sea

The Daring Escape

The Monster Hunt

Journey Through Space

The Thrilling Race

On the Serious Side

Three Ways to Change the World

My Best Friend

The Best Invention Ever

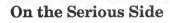

Three Good Rules

An Interesting Hobby

It's Just Not Fair

My Biggest Complaint

On the Silly Side

My Friend the Monster

Stuck in a Sandwich

Ant Goes to School

The Crazy Computer

The World's Longest Worm

The Mouse That Barked

The Cowardly Giant

Mystery

The Case of the Missing Money

Buried Treasure Mystery

The Secret of the Locked Room

The Clue in the Old Castle

The Unknown Student

The Mysterious Stranger

Detective Dan's Famous Case

HOLIDAY HELPERS

HALLOWEEN

The Witch Who Came to Dinner
My Trip to a Haunted House
If I were a ghost I would . . .
The Spookiest Story Ever
The Funniest Costume I Ever Saw
The Pumpkin Nobody Wanted
The Scarecrow That Came to Life

COLUMBUS DAY

My Voyage With Columbus
Columbus was most surprised to discover . . .
One windy day, Columbus got lost at sea

VETERAN'S DAY

The Bravest Soldier Ever
How I Would Put an End to War

HANUKKAH

The Magic Menorah
Eight Special Gifts
Another Hanukkah Miracle

THANKSGIVING

The Fattest Turkey in the World
What the Turkey Told Me
A Colonial Adventure
Life on the Mayflower
The turkey had the silliest stuffing I had ever seen
I looked under Plymouth Rock and was amazed to find . . .
The Best Thanksgiving Memory

CHRISTMAS

Santa got stuck in my chimney
Christmas Eve Surprise
Santa's New Suit
A Visit to Santa's Workshop
The Most Unusual Christmas Gift I Ever Received
My Trip in Santa's Sleigh
One Christmas Eve Rudolph's nose wouldn't shine

NEW YEAR'S

The Day it Rained Confetti
This year I am looking forward to . . .
One Thing I Would Like to Change
When the clock struck midnight,
   the strangest thing happened

VALENTINE'S DAY

The Three People I Love Most
A Valentine Message to My Best Friend
The Silliest Lovebirds
How to Mend a Broken Heart
Cupid shot an arrow and it landed . . .
My heart would break if . . .

ST. PATRICK'S DAY

The Leprechaun's New Home
The Surprise at the End of
   the Rainbow
One day I found a lucky
   shamrock
The Littlest Leprechaun

EASTER

If I had to dye 1,000 eggs . . .
The Bunny That Couldn't Hop
One year the hens couldn't lay eggs

ARBOR DAY

The Most Amazing Treehouse
I couldn't believe what was stuck in the tree
If I could choose a kind of tree to be, I would be . . .

Oodles of Writing Activities © *Edupress*

Time Machine Travels

TO THE PAST

Take a trip back in time and write a story about...

a caveman searching for food
an explorer sent to find new riches for your country
a hunter blazing a trail through an unknown area
a rider for the Pony Express
an invention that changed the world
a voyage around the world with Magellan
a knight fighting a dragon
life in a castle
an adventure on a pirate ship
life in a cave
the first expedition to climb Mt. Everest
a great viking warrior
the land of the dinosaurs
why people thought the world was flat
prospector mining for gold
the discovery of the Antarctic
life without electricity...television...automobiles
the first man to walk on the moon

TO THE FUTURE

Take a trip forward in time and write a story about...

your first trip to Mars
a new way to travel
what you might be doing 20 years from now
a great medical discovery
improvements in the automobile
how telephones might change
planting a farm in outer space
living on a space ship
greatest robot ever
a runaway galaxy
the planet you would like to live on and why
problems of the future (traffic, pollution, etc.)
what it will be like to be a kid 200 years from now
your friend, the extraterrestrial
a startling underwater discovery
a new toy

A Story to finish . . .

The Door to Somewhere

One afternoon my mother sent me on an errand to the grocery store. On my way there, I was sidetracked by the sight of a house that had a newly posted CONDEMNED sign over its front door. Since the house looked fairly new I was instantly curious. I asked a neighbor I saw peeking out the window. He answered in a raspy voice, "Don't go through that door. It leads to somewhere we may not want to know!" Now I was really curious. I stepped up to the front door, put my hand on the knob and _____

_____

_____

_____

_____

_____

_____

_____

_____

_____

Oodles of Writing Activities © *Edupress*

A story to finish . . .

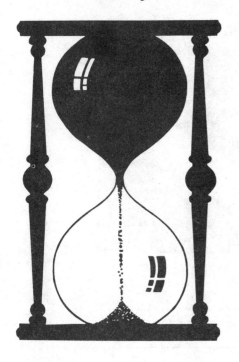

When Time Runs Out

My life as a sailor has had its ups and downs. But as I sit and think of all the memories one particular adventure stands out in my mind.

Our voyage took us across the Atlantic Ocean. A terrible storm hit, our ship was battered and sank. We were lucky to escape with our lives. Or so we thought. We were taken captive by a tribe who took us to their chieftain.

The chieftain told us we could earn our freedom if we could complete a challenge before the sands of time ran out. Little did we know the terrifying challenge that lay before us . . .

_____

_____

_____

_____

_____

_____

_____

_____

_____

_____

Daytime and Nighttime Adventure

• Fold a large piece of paper into four sections. On one section write a story about an adventure you had at night. Here are some suggestions:

> Midnight Mystery
> The Night the Stars Refused to Shine
> A Cry in the Dark

• Opposite the story use crayons to illustrate your story. Press heavily.

• In the third section, write a story about an adventure you had during the day. Here are some suggestions:

> The Unusual Picnic
> Caught in a Snowstorm
> Adventure at Dawn

• Opposite the story use crayons to illustrate your story. Press heavily.

• Finally, use a watercolor wash over each picture—dark blue over the nighttime picture and yellow over the daytime adventure.

Daytime Adventure	
Abcdefgh ijklmnop qr stuvwxyz. Abcd ef ghijklmnop qrs tuv w xyz. Abcd ef g hijk lmnopq r st uvwx yz. Abcde fghij kl m no pqrstuv wxyz. A bc de fghi jklmn opqr stuv wxyz. A bcde fghij lmnopq rst uv wxyz. Abcd efg hijk lmnop qr stu v wxyz. Abcd efgh ij k lm nop qr stu vw xyz.	
Nighttime Adventure	
Abcdefgh ijklmnop qr stuvwxyz. Abcd ef ghijklmnop qrs tuv w xyz. Abcd ef g hijk lmnopq r st uvwx yz. Abcde fghij kl m no pqrstuv wxyz. A bc de fghi jklmn opqr stuv wxyz. A bcde fghij lmnopq rst uv wxyz. Abcd efg hijk lmnop qr stu v wxyz. Abcd efgh ij k lm nop qr stu vw xyz.	

Here are some other story ideas:
   Nighttime Sounds
   Daytime Sounds
   Fun things to do during the daytime/nighttime
   Stories about nocturnal animals—bat, owl, hamster
   Hamster's Big Adventure
   Big Night in the Bat Cave
   What the Owl Learned Last Night

Oodles of Writing Activities © Edupress

Treasure Hunt

Here's a fun-filled buried treasure project!

First write a story about lost treasure. Include details about:

- The legend behind the treasure.

- Who buried it?
    a pirate, an eccentric hermit, an outlaw, a silver prospector?

- What is in the treasure?
    $1,000,000, silver nuggets, gold dubloons, jewelry?

- Where is it hidden?
    in a cave, a secret cove, an abandoned mine shaft?

- How long has the treasure been lost?

- How many attempts have been made to find it? What problems were encountered?

Is your story about a specific attempt to find the treasure? If so . . .

- Who is hunting for it?
    a professional treasure team? three adventuresome boys?

- Describe their search.

- Were they successful?

After the story is written create a treasure map. You can:

Crumple brown wrapping paper
Create a mysterious envelope
Roll it in a rusty jar
Tie up a parchment scroll
Lock it in a box

Be sure the map includes compass directionals, landmarks and written instructions.
For example: *Take 20 paces north from the large oak tree.*

Not all writing comes from your imagination. Often you will need to look in encyclopedias and books for information in order to write a paper or story.

Find three facts about these inventions. Then rewrite the information about each invention on a separate sheet of paper. Add a picture, chart or graph to illustrate the fact.

Put all the pages together in an *Invention Fact Book.*

Just the Facts

Automobile

1. _____

2. _____

3. _____

Telephone

1. _____

2. _____

3. . _____

Airplane

1. _____

2. _____

3. . _____

Radio

1. _____

2. _____

3. _____

Television

1. _____

2. _____

3. _____

More Than a Story

Recipe Card

Write a story about...

- a dinosaur
- with a hungry tummy
- in *your* back yard

Optional ingredients:
stomach ache, non-stop eater, cranky neighbors, food allergies

Activity Menu

Complete one or more of these projects.

❖ Share a book about dinosaurs.

❖ Make a dinosaur stick puppet to "read" your story to your classmates.

❖ Make a magazine picture collage of the food you might have fed to your dinosaur.

❖ Create a picture menu that shows what you fed your dinosaur.

Recipe Card

Write a story about...

- a magician
- on a runaway train
- in the mountains

Optional ingredients:
crazy conductor, passengers, snow, magic tricks

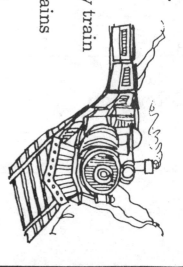

Activity Menu

❖ Use water colors to paint a mountain scene.

❖ Learn and perform a magic trick for classmates.

❖ Draw a picture of what you think the train looked like.

❖ Learn to read a train schedule. (you can get one from a local station or a travel agent.)

Recipe Card

Write a story about...

- a fearless hunter
- in an African jungle
- tracking a very strange animal

Optional ingredients:
native warriors, vines, huge rivers

Activity Menu

✿ Draw or paint a picture of the strange animal you created for your story.

✿ Find actual pictures of two unusual animals.

✿ Bring a book about jungles to share with your classmates.

✿ Create a jungle diorama.

Recipe Card

Write a story about...

- a fairy godmother
- with a brand new wand
- in your classroom

Optional ingredients:
wishes, magic fairy dust, teacher

Activity Menu

★ Make a magic wand by gluing a construction paper star to the end of a paper tube.

★ Draw a picture of the fairy godmother.

★ What do you think "magic fairy dust" looks like? Bring a sample to class. (hint—sugar, glitter, sand, salt)

Write-your-own Recipe Card

- **Story Title**

- **Who—**
- **What—**
- **Where—**

- **Optional Ingredients—**

Write-your-own Recipe Card

- **Story Title**

- **Who—**
- **What—**
- **Where—**

- **Optional Ingredients—**

Write-your-own Recipe Card

- **Story Title**

- **Who—**
- **What—**
- **Where—**

- **Optional Ingredients—**

Write-your-own Recipe Card

- **Story Title**

- **Who—**
- **What—**
- **Where—**

- **Optional Ingredients—**

In My Opinion . . .

Everyone's opinion is worthwhile. But people will listen to your opinion more carefully if you can state very clearly why you feel that way.

First decide if your answer is yes or no. Then list your reasons for choosing that answer. Be sure your reasons make sense.

Should we or shouldn't we . . .
  send a man to Mars
  stop celebrating birthdays
  eat 5 little meals a day instead of 3 big ones
  have homework
  let kids watch television
  have chores to do at home
  share special toys with a friend
  show respect to adults
  ever get in a fight
  fasten our seatbelt in an automobile
  help people in other countries
  have dessert after dinner

Is it or isn't it . . .
  necessary to be rich to be happy
  acceptable to burp at the dinner table
  rude to interrupt if you want to say something
  better to eat peas with a spoon than a fork
  better to have a dog for a pet than a cat
  all right to wipe your mouth clean with your sleeve

Will it or won't it . . .
  hurt your teeth to chew bubblegum
  make a difference if we vote in elections
  make a difference in your grades if you study
  make you more successful if you're pretty or handsome
  be a better world 10 years from now

Just a Short Note

Invitation Information

Design and write an invitation to:

your next birthday party—include time, place, date and theme

a hayride at the local corral

your neighbors for an outdoor barbeque

a Halloween party

a friend from far away to come and stay for a weekend

the wedding of your older sister

a skating party to celebrate Christmas vacation

a "welcome summer" celebration

A Million Thanks

A thank-you note is always welcomed. Write these "make believe" notes:

to your aunt for some new polkadot socks (do you love them?)

to your grandparents for your birthday bicycle

to your neighbor for the cherry pie

to your best friend for helping you with your homework

to your friend's mom for having you to dinner

to your mom and dad for the brand new skateboard (or doll)

to your friend for pet sitting your hamster

Thanks! **Thanks!** **Thanks!** Thanks! **Thanks!**

Greetings!

Design a card and write a short poem, verse or phrase for these occasions:

Congratulations	holiday greetings	Thinking of You
birth of a baby	Christmas	Get Well
graduation	Valentine's Day	Bon Voyage
bar or bat mitzvah	Thanksgiving	a new secret pal
wedding	Mother's Day	a relative's birthday
anniversary	Father's Day	a friend's birthday

Let everyone know about these wonderful (and imaginary) events!

Write an announcement for each. Your announcement can be in poster, flyer, newspaper ad or letter (such as a birth announcement) form. Be sure to include the information listed under the event to be announced.

The Circus is coming!

What dates will it be in town? Where will the big top be? When are the performances? Where can tickets be bought and how much will they be? What will the audience see?

Sign up for Summer Camp

When and where will it be held? How long will the camp session be? How much will it cost? What age children can enroll? What will the kids be doing?

You adopted a pet!

What kind? What is its name? When? Describe the pet.

Announcing the contest winners!

Who won? What did they do to win? What is the prize?

A baby is born!

When? Who are the proud parents? What are the birth statistics (weight, length)? What is the baby's name? Boy or girl?

Grand Opening!

A new store is opening! Where is it? What does it sell? When is the opening? What are the opening specials?

Premiere

What is it (play or movie)? What is the title? Who stars? Where will the premiere be? When?

Not a Story

IN THE NEWS

Try your hand at reporting and writing copy for the newspaper. News stories should include the answers to who, what, when, where and how. Keep this in mind as you write. Include information about dates, places, people and event details.

Choose from these ideas for your first "assignment" as a reporter!

General

World leaders are holding an emergency meeting.
A world-famous person died yesterday.
A Presidential election was held yesterday.
A new law was passed by the state government.
An amazing medical discovery was made.
Dinosaur bones discovered!
Space shuttle launched!
A rare animal was born at the zoo.
Jury hands down surprising verdict.
Lost boat found at sea!
An armored car was robbed!
A big winner was drawn in the lottery.
Cruise ship runs into an iceberg.
There was a giant air disaster.
President makes a startling announcement.

News From the Past
Pretend you are a reporter from the past. Report on these events:

Stagecoach robbed.
Work begins on railroad.
King Arthur slays a dragon.
Columbus discovers America.
Gold is discovered.
A wagon train meets disaster.

Sports

The Super Bowl was played yesterday.
The first game of the World Series was today.
A new record was set in weight lifting.
The Olympics begins.
Baseball player sets a new record.
The heavyweight boxing championship was held last night.
A world-famous car race took place this morning.
Golfers compete for the biggest championship ever.

Entertainment

A new movie is opening this weekend.
A rock star is in town for a concert.
Review the opening of a new restaurant.
Family carnival held this weekend.
New record hits the top of the pop charts.
A surprise winner in the Academy Awards.

Classified Advertising

Check the advertising section of a newspaper before you begin. Ads are short but detailed. When you read the ad back to yourself do you know everything you would need to know if you were the person looking through the ads?

Write an ad for:

Apartment for rent
House for sale
Job offered
Job wanted
Car or truck for sale
A dog you lost
A cat you found
Yard or garage sale (list the items
   you have for sale)
Players wanted for a television game show

Travel Guide

You're a travel agent and it's your job to plan trips for your customers. Plan a trip and create a travel log to present to your customers.

- Include the following information:

    WHERE will they be going? (What country or countries will they visit?)

    HOW many days will they be traveling?

    WHAT kind of transportation—train, riverboat, plane—will they be using?

- Make a packing list—what do they need to bring?

    ...kind of clothing? umbrella? hiking boots? thick socks? evening gown or tuxedo?

- Develop an itinerary—write a schedule for each day's events.

    What will the customer do once the destination is
        reached?
    Will they go horseback riding? skydiving?
        shopping? mountain climbing?

    DESCRIBE where they will
    stay—in a hotel? tent?
    private home?

    INCLUDE some pictures of
    what they might see (to build
    their enthusiasm for the trip!).

    LIST any historical sights
    they will see.

WRITE A LETTER TO . . .

✉ **a child in another country**
Tell him about where you live. Ask him about where he lives.

✉ **a newspaper editor**
Comment on something in your community. Make a suggestion for something you would like to see changed.

✉ **a children's magazine**
Share a poem or a story about yourself.

✉ **your mom, dad, grandma, aunt, uncle, cousin (and so on)**
Tell them what's happening in your life.

✉ **the principal of your school**
Tell her what you think she's doing right. Tell her what you would like to have different.

✉ **the President of your country**
Tell him what you like best about living in your country. Tell him one thing you would like to see him improve.

✉ **a government official**
Ask her how she would vote on a particular issue. Tell her how you think she should vote.

✉ **a secret pal**
Share a secret. Give him a clue as to who you are.

✉ **someone who's sick**
Say something to cheer him up.

✉ **an elderly person in a retirement home**
Tell a funny story about something you did that day.

OTHER KINDS OF LETTERS . . .

letter of complaint	placing an order
introduction	thank you
request	business

From Tiny Acorns
Look what you can do with just one word!

Dinosaur

1. Write 5 words describing how you would feel if you met a dinosaur one day.
2. List 3 places a dinosaur could not fit into.
3. List 3 places a dinosaur could fit.
4. List 10 things a dinosaur might keep in its refrigerator.
5. Describe where a dinosaur might sleep.
6. For each letter in the word dinosaur, write a word or phrase that relates. (example: d=dreaded, i=inept, n=not nimble, etc.)
7. What would you do with a dinosaur that came to school?
8. Write 3 questions you would like to ask a dinosaur.
9. See #6 above. Write a sentence for each word or phrase.
10. What do you think would scare a dinosaur?

Astronaut

1. Write 3 things an astronaut might do.
2. List 5 words relating to an astronaut.
3. Make a list of things an astronaut should take to Mars.
4. Make a list of the qualities an astronaut should have.
5. Tell whether or not you would want to be an astronaut and why.
6. Write a note to an astronaut.
7. Describe what the astronaut saw outside his spaceship.
8. Write how you think it would feel to walk on the moon.
9. Draw an "*astroknot..*"
10. How would you hold down a weightless astronaut?

Huge

1. Write a huge word.
2. Make up a huge lie.
3. How would you dig a huge hole?
4. Tell three problems a huge person might have.
5. What is the hugest thing you can think of?
6. Tell about a huge problem you have.
7. List as many huge animals as you can.
8. Write a story about the day you had to eat a huge donut.
9. Write a sentence with the word huge in it . . .all the other words must start with the letter "h".
10. How many people do you think are in a huge crowd? What would they be doing?

Dare and Do

Write "dares" for your classmates. These dares cannot be dangerous. Put all the dares into a large jar. Take them out during spare class moments and ask volunteers to attempt the dare.

The "dares" should be fun. The sillier the better! For example:

"I dare someone to stand on their hands for five seconds."

"I dare someone to sing a song in front of the class."

"I dare someone to put a book on their head and walk to the principal's office without dropping it."

"I dare someone to keep a straight face while the rest of the class makes silly faces.

OR devote a day to DARE AND DO. Here are some activities:

- Write a story about a daring accomplishment.

- Research daring accomplishments. Learn about the first person to climb Mt. Whitney. Research the first flight into space.

- Keep a record book of daring accomplishments. On Dare and Do Day see what accomplishments can be topped.

- Divide into teams. Each team accepts the same dare. For example:

    Which team can go the longest without speaking?
    Which team can make the tallest stack of books without any falling?
    Which team can get the most clothespins in the jar?

Direction Connection

Write complete directions for some of the following:

Going places

How could someone get...
   from school to your house
   from your classroom to the restroom
   from your desk to the pencil sharpener
   from your house to the market
   from your country to another
   from your house to your grandmother's
   from your classroom to the principal's office
   from your house to the nearest park or playground

Assembly line

How to put together...
   a model airplane
   a go-cart
   a jigsaw puzzle
   a bicycle

Food stuff

Tell how to make...
   a peanut butter and jelly sandwich
   lemonade
   pancakes
   a hamburger
   cereal in a bowl
   popcorn
   jello
   a tossed green salad
   a hot fudge sundae

Doing things

Steps for...
   making a bed
   putting on a blouse or shirt
   walking a dog
   putting on a pair of your shoes
   planting a flower
   pitching a tent
   building a fire
   buying a ticket at the movies
   wrapping a present
   taking a picture
   painting a picture